W9-CDW-562

INTO THE WOODS
Exploring the Forest Ecosystem

INTO THE WOODS

Exploring the Forest Ecosystem

LAURENCE PRINGLE

MACMILLAN PUBLISHING CO., INC.
New York
COLLIER MACMILLAN PUBLISHERS
London

Macmillan Publishing Co., Inc., 866 Third Avenue, New York, N.Y. 10022
Collier-Macmillan Canada Ltd., Toronto, Ontario

Library of Congress catalog card number: 72–92448
Printed in the United States of America
10 9 8 7 6 5 4 3 2 1

Library of Congress Cataloging in Publication Data

Pringle, Laurence P   Into the woods: exploring the forest ecosystem.

Bibliography: p.   1. Forest ecology—Juvenile literature.
[1. Forest ecology. 2. Ecology]   I. Title.
QH541.5.F6P74   574.5′264   72–92448   ISBN 0–02–775320–4

*For Charles Oestreicher,
who helped me out of the woods*

ABOUT THIS BOOK

A forest is one kind of ecosystem—a place in nature with all of its living and nonliving parts. Ecosystems are all around us. Some are big, some are little. The planet earth is one ecosystem, a rotting log is another. Ponds, fields, and backyards are also ecosystems.

This book introduces forest ecosystems. Forests cover nearly a third of the land on earth. Some forests are made up of trees only 25 feet tall; others have trees ten times higher. There are about 25 major types of forests in the United States, and many more around the globe.

Some forests have been destroyed and nearly all have been changed in some way by people. But forests are still among the most valuable ecosystems on earth. They provide wood for building, making paper, and many other uses. They provide nuts, fruit, and other food. They protect water supplies and soil by soaking up water from rain and melting snow. They are homes for deer, squirrels, and many other animals. And in a noisy, crowded world, forests are quiet, beautiful places where people can relax.

Although there are many different kinds of forests around the world, most of them are alike in some ways. As you explore a little woods in your neighborhood, you will find similarities to great forests on other continents. Through your observations and through the pages of this book, you can begin to know the fascinating ecosystem of the forest.

A forest is cool, green, and dark. It can be a scary place if you have always lived in a city. For most people, though, a forest seems friendly and inviting. It is a fascinating place to explore.

A forest is especially inviting on a hot summer day. The sun beats down as you cross a field to reach the woods. Then you are among the trees. You feel cooler.

At first the forest seems like a jumble of trees, bushes, and other plants. Look around, and you may see that the plants grow in layers.

The canopy is high above your head. It is made up of the leafy crowns of the tallest trees. The canopy can be anywhere from 25 to 250 feet high, depending on the kinds of trees and their ages.

The understory is below the canopy. It is made up of young trees that will grow taller and types of trees that normally do not grow very high. Usually part of the understory is the canopy of the future. As the tall canopy trees die or are cut down, the young trees of the understory replace them.

A view from the canopy shows
young trees, shrubs, and herbs
growing from the forest floor.

CANOPY

UNDER-
STORY

SHRUB
LAYER

HERB LAYER

DECIDUOUS FOREST—
EASTERN NORTH AMERICA

Shrubs grow beneath the understory. They are bushy plants that have many woody stems. In some kinds of forests, especially dense evergreen forests, there may be so little light that no shrubs can grow. In more open forests, shrubs may be so abundant that they are hard to walk through.

Plants called herbs grow at your feet. Herbs are green plants with soft stems. Most forest wildflowers are herbs. The herb layer also includes other low-growing plants, including mosses, ferns, and mushrooms.

Underfoot is the forest floor. In most forests it is carpeted with fallen leaves. The forest floor is a sort of wastebasket for all the layers of plants above. Each year in eastern North America, about ten million leaves fall onto an acre of forest floor.

Few plants grow in the dim light beneath dense evergreens (right).

Sit in the dim coolness and look up at the canopy. It looks warm and sunny up there. Wind may be blowing limbs and leaves about, even though you feel only a slight breeze where you sit on the forest floor. Each of the different layers of forest plant life has its own climate (the average temperature, wind, rainfall, and other weather an area has over the years).

The trees that make up a forest have a remarkable effect on its climate. Most of the sunlight that shines on a sidewalk or field never reaches the ground in a forest. Some sunlight is reflected from the top of the canopy. A lot is soaked up by the canopy leaves. Only a small amount of sunlight reaches the understory. And in some forests, less than one one-hundredth of the sunlight reaches the forest floor.

The amount of sunlight at different levels of the forest affects the air temperature. High in the treetops, the temperature may be 95° Fahrenheit or higher. At the shady forest floor, it may only be 70°F. At night the canopy cools, and the temperature is about the same throughout the forest.

The canopy in an
eastern deciduous forest

Trees have other effects on a forest's climate. The strong winds that whip across open fields are slowed to a gentle breeze within the woods. When rain beats down on open land, it loosens soil and may wash it away. In the woods, the raindrops from a shower may not even reach the soil. They are caught in the umbrella of the canopy. Many drops cling to leaves, twigs, and bark. Most of these drops eventually escape into the air as water vapor. Some raindrops drip gently to the understory and then to the forest floor. A few drops from a rain shower may soak into the rotting leaves that carpet the ground. When lots of rain falls, the water trickles slowly through the spongy layers of dead leaves and soaks in the ground below.

Layers of leaves on the forest floor soak up raindrops and protect the soil below.

Each layer of plant life is different from the others in many ways. Because of these differences, each is the home for different kinds of animals.

Some animals are born, live, and die in just one layer of forest plant life. Others may be found in all layers. Some catch food in one layer and make their nest or den in another. In most forests, you will find the greatest variety of life in the herb and forest-floor layers. Many forest insects spend part of their lives on or beneath the forest floor.

Other kinds of animals live high in the canopy. There is plenty of food there for plant-eating insects. Caterpillars and leaf miners chew on leaves, while aphids and leafhoppers suck leaf juices.

Leaf-eating caterpillars (left) are caught in the canopy by crested flycatchers (right).

The insect life in the canopy attracts insect-eating birds. Scarlet tanagers flash high overhead, catching insects to feed to their young in nests which may be 50 feet above ground. Flycatchers, vireos, and cerulean warblers also feed in the canopy.

The canopy is a safe refuge for crows, hawks, and owls. These big birds usually build nests in canopy trees where it is difficult for a raccoon, human, or other enemy to reach their eggs or young.

Blue jays eat acorns in the canopy but also feed on the forest floor. They build their nests in the understory.

You may see squirrels in all layers of the forest. They eat seeds, buds, and nuts in the canopy and often build their nests there. They also forage on the ground, and bury nuts beneath the forest floor. At night, flying squirrels climb tree trunks up into the canopy. Then they may glide a hundred feet or more, landing on another tree or on the ground. They eat seeds, nuts, and insects they find in trees and on the forest floor.

Many birds nest and hunt for food in the understory and shrub layers. Insects are plentiful there, and spiders spin wheel-shaped webs which trap moths and other flying insects. Chipmunks sometimes climb small trees and shrubs to find seeds and berries. Deer eat the buds and stems of these plants, too.

Flying insects are caught in the webs of forest spiders (top). Flying squirrels (bottom) are active at night. By spreading loose flaps of skin between their front and rear legs, they are able to glide through the air.

In most forests, life is especially abundant among the herbs and on the forest floor. Wildflowers brighten the leaf-covered earth. Many of these plants grow and bloom in the spring in non-evergreen forests, when plenty of sunlight reaches the ground. The leaves of wildflowers use sun energy and change some of it to food energy. Some of the food energy is stored in their roots. By late spring, when the canopy leaves are fully grown, very little sunlight reaches the plants on the forest floor. The leaves and stems of many wildflowers die. Their roots live on, waiting for another spring.

Animal trails weave in and out among the plants of the herb layer. Many forest mammals are active at dawn and dusk. Then the trails are traveled by foxes, deer, skunks, opossums, and bobcats. Mice and shrews scurry along the forest floor. If you sit still in a forest at night, you will hear little rustlings in the leaves. A twig snaps behind you. Thump —a flying squirrel lands on a nearby tree trunk. Mammals are on the move all around you.

Canada Mayflower often grows in a thick carpet on the forest floor.

Many forest mammals sleep by day, but other kinds of animals are awake. Box turtles look among the herbs for berries, insects, and snails to eat. Snakes slither along on the leaves, and salamanders creep out of their dark hiding places. A toad hops among the ferns or sits and waits for a mosquito to fly near. In a flash the toad's tongue lashes out and snares the insect.

Some kinds of birds spend most of their lives among the herbs and other low-growing plants on the forest floor. They eat insects and other small animals, and almost never fly more than a few feet above the ground (except while migrating). Their nests are usually hidden among the leaves and herbs. One bird is named for its well-hidden nest. This is the ovenbird, whose nest is arched over with a protective cover of leaves. It has a side entrance and looks like a small oven.

*Snails feed on the detritus of the
forest floor, while garter snakes catch
mice and other small animals there.*

On top of the leaves of the forest floor you may see other creatures—daddy longlegs, ants, wood frogs. But many more animals live underneath. Lift away some of the leaves. It is cool, damp, and dark under them. You may find an earthworm, the larvae (young) of a beetle, or some sow bugs (which are more closely related to crabs than to insects).

Dig deeper through the layers of leaves. You may not be able to tell exactly where the leaves end and the soil begins. Between the partly decayed leaves and the soil is a layer called humus. It is especially rich with life. Humus is made up of bits of leaves which are so decayed that they may be too tiny to see.

Each layer of leaves is more decayed than the one above it. The bottommost layers are called humus, and are just above the top of the soil.

For each living animal or plant you see, there are billions more that can only be seen with a microscope. In a square foot of forest floor, three inches deep, there may be as many as a hundred billion organisms. Most are tiny plants called fungi and bacteria. Some are microscopic animals called protozoa. The protozoa and some other animals are water creatures. They live in water-filled spaces between bits of leaves or in the thin film of water that coats soil particles.

The forest floor is an ideal living place, or habitat, for these tiny animals and plants. They could not live in a drier, sunnier place. And there is plenty of food. Most of the food energy of the forest comes from the leaves of plants. Part of the sun energy that strikes living leaves is changed into food energy. This food-making process is called photosynthesis, which means "putting together with light." Plants use some food energy to make more food and to make new leaves, stems, roots, and seeds. Insects get some energy as they feed on the plants. Birds and squirrels get energy from the insects, seeds, and berries they eat. But huge amounts of food energy also reach the forest floor as the dead leaves drift down in the autumn.

Protozoa like these live in tiny bits of water within the soil and among the dead leaves on the forest floor.

THREE MAJOR GROUPS OF PROTOZOANS

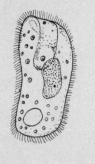

CILIATES

SARCODINIANS

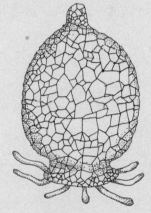

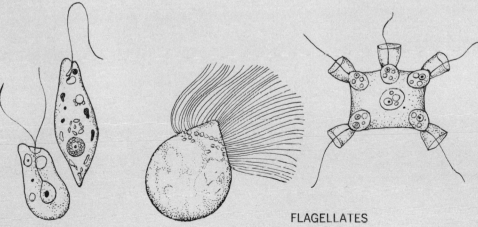

FLAGELLATES

Photo courtesy of the American Museum of Natural History

Leaves, twigs, fruits, seeds, parts of flowers, the bodies of insects and other animals—all eventually become part of the forest floor. Nearly two tons of this dead material, or detritus, may fall onto an acre in a year.

The forest doesn't choke on its detritus though. All of the dead things are broken down, or decayed, by forest-floor animals and especially by bacteria and fungi. Earthworms can eat freshly fallen leaves. Other animals, such as mites, millipedes, sow bugs, and springtails, eat leaves after they have been softened and partly decayed. Millipedes, mites, and springtails also eat bacteria and fungi.

As much as 95 percent of the energy in a forest is used by plants and animals like these. That means just 5 percent is left for animals like squirrels and deer—the ones we usually think are the important forest animals. Tiny creatures like springtails may be more important in the energy flow of forests.

Thousands of springtails may live in just a small area of forest floor. They eat decaying leaves. They are hunted by spiders and centipedes. Springtails have a springlike escape device on the underside of their bodies. It flings them as far as four inches through the air—a great leap for an animal that is only an eighth of an inch long.

This enlarged view of a bit of forest floor, part of a museum exhibit, shows a millipede, sow bug, and springtail (lower right).

Because bacteria and fungi cause dead things to decay, they are called decomposers. Fungi are the most important decomposers in forests. They break down parts of wood that bacteria cannot decay. Most parts of fungus plants are tiny and hidden from sight. There may be miles and miles of slender fungal strands in a small area of forest floor.

Usually all you see of these important plants are their spore-producing parts—mushrooms or toadstools. They often pop up overnight—strange, colorful shapes on logs and on the forest floor. They soon die, but not before releasing hundreds of millions of spores which drift through the air. When a spore lands in a dark, wet place, it grows into another spreading fungus plant.

The small animals of the forest floor chew and grind up bits of leaves. When they die, their bodies are eaten by still smaller animals, or are broken down further by fungi and bacteria. Bit by bit, all of the leaves, twigs, and other detritus are decayed. Eventually all that remains are elements such as nitrogen, iron, and calcium. These nutrients are needed for the growth of all living things.

Fungi get their food from dead trees and other plant material. The mushrooms that sprout from logs are only a small part of the fungus plants within the decaying wood.

Nutrients are carried down into the soil by water from rain or melting snow. The water seeps among the soil particles and along passageways dug by earthworms, insect larvae, and other animals. Air also flows into the earth and reaches roots in this way. The tunnels and burrows of soil animals are important to the life of forest plants.

Underground, the nutrients cling to soil particles. If you dig into the humus and the soil you can figure out what happens to the nitrogen and other elements that come from detritus. You will find the roots of wildflowers, young trees, and even the roots of the trees that tower overhead. The plant roots take the nutrients from the soil.

Along with water, the nutrients are taken into a tree's roots and then carried up the tree. They become part of the trunk, branches, twigs, flowers, and leaves. Later the leaves and other parts die and fall to the ground. Their death brings new life to the forest floor. The process of decay continues day and night, releasing new supplies of nutrients for the life of the forest.

Air and water flow into the soil through earthworm tunnels. The worms also mix bits of leaves with the minerals of forest soils.

Thousands of years ago, half of the land on earth was covered by forests. Since then people have cleared away many forests to make way for cities and farms. Forests now cover about a third of the land. The earth's forests are made up of many different kinds of trees, and different kinds of animals live in them. But all forests are alike in some ways.

This forest in New York's Adirondack Mountains

Some are made up entirely of deciduous or broadleaf trees—those that lose all of their leaves once a year. Others are made up of coniferous trees. They lose their leaves too, but not all at once, so they are called evergreens. Their leaves, called needles, decay more slowly than the leaves of deciduous trees.

is a mixture of coniferous and deciduous trees.

The climate of an area has a great effect on the kind of forest that grows there, or whether a forest can exist at all. There is too little rain in deserts and on prairies to support forests. In places where rain is plentiful, forests grow thick and tall. One forest of this kind grows along the northwest coast of North America, from Alaska to northern California. It is called the temperate rain forest. As much as 140 inches of rain fall on the forest each year. (This is about 100 inches more precipitation than falls on forests in the northeastern and north central United States.) The rain drips gently down through tall evergreens onto a forest floor covered with thick growths of mosses and ferns.

At the southern end of this rainy area, close to the sea, live the tallest trees in the world—the coast redwoods. The redwood forest grows on a narrow, 450-mile-long strip, never out of reach of summer fogs that drift in from the ocean. The lowest limbs of a redwood may be a hundred feet above ground, and the treetop 350 feet high.

The redwood forest at Muir Woods
National Monument in California

Many tourists visit this tropical rain forest in Puerto Rico.

Another kind of rain forest grows around the middle of the earth. This tropical rain forest grows in Central America, in the Amazon Basin of South America, in Africa, Malaya, New Guinea, and the Philippines. Rain forests have a layer of plant life that is missing in other forests. Some giant trees rise above the main canopy.

Woody vines hang from the rain-forest trees. Some are as thick as a man's waist. Their leaves make up part of the canopy. Smaller plants, some of them related to cacti, grow on the limbs of canopy trees. Usually the canopy is so leafy that very little sunlight reaches the forest floor. Only a few plants grow there.

The ground is often bare of dead leaves. The tropical climate is ideal for animals, bacteria, and fungi. Anything that dies decays quickly. Just as quickly, most of the nutrients become part of living plants. In tropical rain forests, unlike most other forests, very little food energy and nutrients are tied up in dead leaves and soil.

TROPICAL RAIN FOREST

31

The rain-forest canopy is a lively place. Monkeys, lemurs, and sloths live there. So do many kinds of bats, birds, frogs, snakes, lizards, and insects. The forest teems with life, but most of the animals are hidden from sight in the canopy. Many are active only at night.

Of all forests, the tropical rain forest is most easily harmed by people. In other forests, great amounts of nutrients are stored in the detritus and the soil. When trees are cut down or burned, there are still plenty of nutrients available for new growth. A rain forest's nutrients, however, are mostly stored in living plants. When trees are cut and burned, almost all of the forest's nitrogen, sulfur, and carbon goes up in smoke and gases. The regular rains of the tropics carry other nutrients deep into the soil, beyond the reach of roots. Some nutrients are left, but they are quickly used up as farmers harvest a crop or two. Then the soil is "worn out" and has to be abandoned.

Weeds and vines take over the fields. Eventually trees grow there again. But a long time—perhaps 200 years—is needed for the return of the true rain forest, with its full variety of plants and animals.

Both the silver leaf monkey (top)
and the slow loris (bottom)
live in tropical rain forests.

When eastern North America was first settled by Europeans, millions of acres of forest were cleared for farming. Later many people moved to cities, abandoning their farms. Grasses and weeds sprang up. Young trees grew from roots in the ground or from seeds blown by the wind from nearby woods, or carried in accidentally by animals. The first plants to grow were kinds that thrive in open, sunny fields. They were gradually replaced by slower-growing plants that could survive in shade. As young trees grew, their shade kept sunlight from reaching grasses and other field plants. These plants died and were replaced by forest shrubs and herbs. After fifty years or more, a forest covered the land where corn or wheat once grew.

This process is called plant succession. You can see it going on all around you—in fields, in city lots, along roadsides. Look in these places and you will probably find young trees growing among weeds and grasses. If the trees are left undisturbed, they will someday be part of a forest.

A young maple tree in a meadow
may someday be part of a forest.

Forest fires have always been a normal happening in the dry forests of southern California.

Plant succession also takes place after a forest fire, or after a forest is felled by lumberjacks. Sunlight floods the forest floor. Trees and shrubs sprout from seeds and roots in the soil. A new forest rises from the ashes of the old.

When European settlers first came to North America, they found vast stretches of forest. But they also found grassy meadows and young forests. These were the results of forest fires caused by lightning and set on purpose by Indians. The Indians knew that certain plants, such as raspberries, and

certain animals, such as deer, are more plentiful in open country and in young forests than in fully grown forests.

A forest fire in the woods *can* do great damage. It may kill trees and destroy the habitat of wild animals. It often leaves the ground bare and unprotected from rain that washes soil away. People have learned of the dangers of forest fires and try to prevent them. Fewer acres of woods burn each year, even though more people use forests for hiking, camping, and other recreation.

However, foresters have learned that fire sometimes helps certain kinds of trees to grow and reproduce. They have also learned that a series of mild fires over the years burns away some of the detritus and so prevents one huge fire and the damage it could do. So foresters sometimes set fires on purpose, just as Indians once did. By choosing a time a few days after a rain, and when there is little wind, they are able to keep the fire under control. These conditions also help keep the fire from producing as much heat and damage as a forest fire out of control.

Many coniferous trees have thick bark and can live through the heat of a small fire. Several valuable evergreens reproduce themselves best after a forest fire. These trees include Douglas fir, the leading source of lumber in the United States, and southern yellow pine, the main source of wood for making paper.

A forester setting a fire among loblolly pines in South Carolina

The seed-bearing cones of some pine trees need heat in order to open and release their seeds. Jack pine, a tree used for making paper and boxes, has cones which pop open at 122° F. If jack pine seeds fall upon a thick layer of dead leaves and other detritus, very few of them sprout and grow. They grow best where there is bare soil or an inch or two of detritus. After a fire, jack pine seeds fall onto ground where most of the detritus has been burned away—ideal conditions for them.

Forests in North America have survived fires for many thousands of years. Some forests seem to need regular fires for their own good. Of course, people should still be careful with matches and campfires, to avoid setting a forest fire. But foresters will continue to study the effects of fires on forests, and may set greater numbers of controlled fires in the future.

Forest fires can do great damage, but some kinds of trees reproduce themselves best after a fire. The photo on the right shows seeds falling from a jack pine cone which was opened by the heat of a forest fire.

Just as ideas about forest fires are changing, so are other ideas about how we use forests. This is especially true of the national forests—154 forests that cover 181 million acres in the United States. Most of them are in eleven western states. Private companies pay the government for the right to cut timber from them.

The national forests, however, belong to all of the people. The forests are supposed to have many uses, including camping, hiking, hunting, fishing, and protection of water supplies. They are supposed to provide habitats for wildlife. They are supposed to be well cared for, so that future generations can enjoy them too.

People use forests for all sorts of recreation, including camping and hiking.

Many people believe that the national forests are not being used properly. Foresters are far behind in their efforts to replant and care for areas where all of the trees were cut down. Logging in some forests has left steep slopes unprotected from rain. Soil has washed into rivers and other streams, destroying the places where trout and salmon used to breed. Many people believe that the officials in charge of the national forests are neglecting the many uses of these woods in favor of one use—growing wood for sale. People are working to make sure that the national forests will be better cared for in the future.

As the number of people on earth increases, the need for food, fuel, lumber, paper, and wildlife from forests also grows. Scientists are trying to learn more about forests in order to use them more wisely. They are studying ways of cutting timber without causing a great loss of soil or nutrients. They are also trying new ways of adding more nutrients to forests. One idea that is being tested is to fertilize woods with ground-up bits of garbage from cities.

In their efforts to cut more timber for sale, foresters have harmed some national forests and lessened their usefulness for recreation, wildlife habitat, and soil protection.

In recent years, hundreds of scientists have been studying forests in North America and elsewhere in the world. They have already made some important discoveries. They discovered that dead roots in the soil are an important source of nutrients for living plants. They were surprised at the great amount of oxygen—a gas needed by nearly all living things—given off by scattered forests in the northeastern United States, where so many people live.

These findings help us to better understand forests. Knowing more about forests, we can take better care of them. Then we will always have these places of mystery and beauty to explore and enjoy.

GLOSSARY

BACTERIA—tiny one-celled plants that cannot make their own food, and get it from other living or dead organisms. Bacteria aid the decay of dead plants and animals.

CANOPY—the topmost layer of plant life in a forest, formed by the leaves and branches of the tallest trees.

CLIMATE—the average weather conditions of an area, including temperature, windiness, the amount of rain and other precipitation, the amount of water vapor in the air, and the hours of sunlight.

CONIFER—a plant that bears its seeds in cones. A conifer is usually a tree with needlelike leaves. Most coniferous trees are evergreens, losing their needles gradually rather than all at once. See DECIDUOUS.

DECIDUOUS—a plant that periodically loses all of its leaves, usually in the autumn. A few conifers, such as larch and cypress, are also deciduous.

DECOMPOSERS—microscopic organisms (bacteria, yeast, and fungi) that feed upon once-living material and cause it to break down or decay.

DETRITUS—bits and pieces of anything; in a forest, bits and pieces of dead plants and animals on the forest floor.

ECOLOGY—the study of relationships between living things and their environment.

ECOSYSTEM—a place in nature with all of its living and nonliving parts, including soils and climate. The earth is one huge ecosystem. Other ecosystems include forests, deserts, ponds, puddles, and rotting logs.

ELEMENT—a distinct kind of matter consisting of atoms of only one kind. It cannot be broken down by ordinary chemical or physical processes. Examples include oxygen, calcium, iron, hydrogen, lead.

FOREST FLOOR—the layer of decaying detritus that covers the soil in a forest.

FUNGI—a group of plants that, like bacteria, cannot make their own food. Fungi include yeasts, molds, and mushrooms. They aid the decay of dead plants and animals.

HABITAT—the living place, or immediate surroundings, of an organism.

HERB—any flowering plant that has a soft, rather than woody, stem.

HUMUS—bits of decayed detritus so small that they are no longer recognizable as leaves or other dead material. On the forest floor there is a layer of humus between the layers of dead leaves and the minerals of the soil.

LARVAE—the young of some groups of animals, especially insects. Larvae are usually quite active; a caterpillar is the larva of a butterfly.

NUTRIENT—a substance needed for normal growth and development of an organism.

PHOTOSYNTHESIS—the process in green plants in which light energy from the sun is changed into chemical (food) energy in the form of simple sugars.

PLANT SUCCESSION—the process of gradual replacement of one community of plants by another over a period of time. Each community of plants has certain animals in it, and they change as the plant life changes. Over most of North America, the final stage of plant succession is a forest.

PROTOZOA—one-celled microscopic animals. Protozoa include amoebas, stentors, and radiolarians.

SHRUBS—woody plants that are usually less than twelve feet tall and that have more than one stem rising from the ground.

SPORES—the reproductive cells of such plants as ferns, mosses, molds, and mushrooms.

UNDERSTORY—the layer of plant life formed by the crowns of the smaller trees of a forest.

FURTHER READING

Books marked with an asterisk (*) are fairly simple; the others are more difficult.

BROCKMAN, C. FRANK. *Trees of North America: A Field Guide to the Major Native and Introduced Species North of Mexico.* New York: Golden Press, 1968.

FARB, PETER, and THE EDITORS OF LIFE. *The Forest.* New York: Time, Inc., 1963; revised, 1971.

FROME, MICHAEL. *The Forest Service.* New York: Praeger, 1971.

*KANE, HENRY B. *Four Seasons in the Woods.* New York: Knopf, 1968.

*———. *The Tale of a Wood.* New York: Knopf, 1962.

*McCORMICK, JACK. *The Life of the Forest.* New York: McGraw-Hill, 1966.

*MILNE, LORUS and MARGERY. *Because of a Tree.* New York: Atheneum, 1963.

*PRINGLE, LAURENCE, ed. *Discovering the Outdoors: A Nature and Science Guide to Investigating Life in Fields, Forests, and Ponds.* New York: Natural History Press, 1969.

*———. *Ecology: Science of Survival.* New York: Macmillan, 1971.

*RICHARDS, PAUL. *The Life of the Jungle.* New York: McGraw-Hill, 1970.

*SELSAM, MILLICENT. *See Through the Forest.* New York: Harper & Row, 1956.

*SIMON, SEYMOUR. *A Handful of Soil.* New York: Hawthorn, 1970.

*ZIM, HERBERT, and ALEXANDER MARTIN. *Trees: A Golden Nature Guide.* New York: Golden Press, 1963.

INDEX

*Asterisk (*) indicates drawing or photograph*

PICTURE CREDITS

National Audubon Society, 9 (O. S. Pettingill, Jr.), 11 bottom (Leonard Lee Rue), 33 top (Karl Kenyon), 33 bottom (Gordon Smith); Packaging Corporation of America, 41 (John Calkins); Laurence Pringle, cover, i, title page, v, vi, viii, 3, 4, 7, 8, 11 top, 12, 14, 15, 17, 23 top, 23 bottom, 24, 26–27, 34, 42, 43, 47, 48, 52; Sierra Club, 44 (Gordon Robinson); U.S. Department of Agriculture: Forest Service, 30 (P. Freeman Heim), 36–37 (F. E. Dunham), 39 (Daniel O. Todd), 40 (Bluford W. Muir); U.S. Department of the Interior: National Park Service, 29 (George A. Grant).

Drawings on pages 2, 19, and 31 by Ray Skibinski

ALSO BY LAURENCE PRINGLE

FOR YOUNG READERS

Dinosaurs and Their World

The Only Earth We Have

From Field to Forest

In a Beaver Valley

One Earth, Many People:
  The Challenge of Human Population Growth

Cockroaches:
  Here, There, and Everywhere

Ecology:
  Science of Survival

From Pond to Prairie

This Is a River

Pests and People:
  The Search for Sensible Pest Control

Estuaries:
  Where Rivers Meet the Sea

FOR ADULTS

Wild River

The Date Due Card in the pocket indicates the date on or before which this
book should be returned to the Library.

Please do not remove cards from this
pocket.